LIZARDS

by Tanya Lee Stone

BLACKBIRCH®
PRESS

THOMSON

GALE

San Diego • Detroit • New York • San Francisco • Cleveland • New Haven, Conn. • Waterville, Maine • London • Munich

© 2003 by Blackbirch Press™. Blackbirch Press™ is an imprint of The Gale Group, Inc., a division of Thomson Learning, Inc.

Blackbirch Press™ and Thomson Learning™ are trademarks used herein under license.

For more information, contact
The Gale Group, Inc.
27500 Drake Rd.
Farmington Hills, MI 48331-3535
Or you can visit our Internet site at http://www.gale.com

Photographs © 2001 by Xiang Gao-Shi

Cover Photograph © PhotoDisc

Illustration by Yan Kai-Xin

© 2001 by Chin-Chin Publications Ltd.

No. 274-1, Sec.1 Ho-Ping E. Rd., Taipei, Taiwan, R.O.C.
Tel: 886-2-2363-3486 Fax: 886-2-2363-6081

Dedication: For Jake and Liza

LIBRARY OF CONGRESS CATALOGING-IN-PUBLICATION DATA

Stone, Tanya Lee.
  Lizards / by Tanya Lee Stone.
    v. cm. -- (Wild wild world)
  Includes bibliographical references.
  Contents: Many kinds -- Meat-eaters -- Mating -- Dangers.
  ISBN 1-4103-0052-8 (hardback : alk. paper)
  1. Lizards--Juvenile literature. [1. Lizards.] I. Title. II. Series.

  QL666.L2J23 2003
  597.95--dc21

                                                              2003001487

Printed in Taiwan
10 9 8 7 6 5 4 3 2 1

Table of Contents

About Lizards

There are thousands of different kinds of lizards in many colors and sizes. Lizards are reptiles. They live mainly on land in warm areas all over the world. Most have four legs and sharp teeth. They also have long tails, dry scaly skin, and five clawed toes on each foot. Lizards don't have ears that you can see. They have ear openings.

Most lizards have keen eyesight. They blink their eyelids to keep their eyes clean. They also have a clear membrane that helps protect their eyes.

Lizards smell and taste using their tongue.

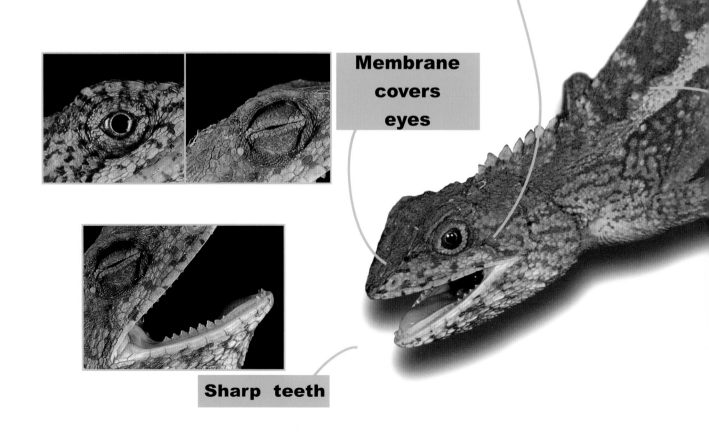

Ear opening

Membrane covers eyes

Sharp teeth

4

Long tail

Five clawed toes on each foot

Dry, scaly skin

Incredible Climbers

Lizards are fast movers and incredible climbers! They run, climb, and cling to surfaces.

Lizards can move over most anything in their way. Logs, rocks, and even buildings don't stop them. They run straight up and down trees! Some lizards can even raise their upper bodies off the ground and run on two legs.

Lizards use their long tails for balance. Some lizards have tails designed for grasping tree branches. The claws on their feet also help them climb. Certain lizards, such as geckos, have tiny hooks on their feet that help them climb very smooth surfaces.

Cold-Blooded Animals

Like all reptiles, lizards are cold-blooded. That means the temperature of their body changes with the temperature of the environment around them. Being cold-blooded helps reptiles save energy so they can survive when food is hard to find.

To warm up, lizards lie in the sun. To cool down, they find shade by crawling under a rock or into a burrow.

Can you spot the lizard in the tree on page 9?

Swift Hunters

Most lizards are meat-eaters. They are swift hunters. Lizards can snatch up insects with their mouths and claws. Many lizards also eat birds, small mammals, and even other reptiles. Some kinds of lizards only eat fruits and other plant foods. Lizards use teeth in their upper and lower jaws to crush their food.

Many lizards have patterns and colorings that allow them to blend into the surroundings. Some lizards, such as chameleons, can actually change colors. Being hard to see helps lizards hide from enemies. It also helps them sneak up on their prey without being noticed.

Defending Territory

Male lizards will defend their territory. If another male comes too close, two males may fight.

Before fighting, each male will try to scare the other. To do this, a male may open its mouth or make a hissing sound. Sometimes a male will puff himself up with air. This makes him appear bigger.

Mating

During mating season, lizards have different ways to attract a mate. Some males wrestle or fight with each other to "win" a female. Many male lizards change color during mating season. Others do a courtship "dance" or chase a female to get her attention.

The opening to a lizard's reproductive system is under the base of its tail. This opening is called the cloaca. To mate, male and female lizards need to connect at their cloacas.

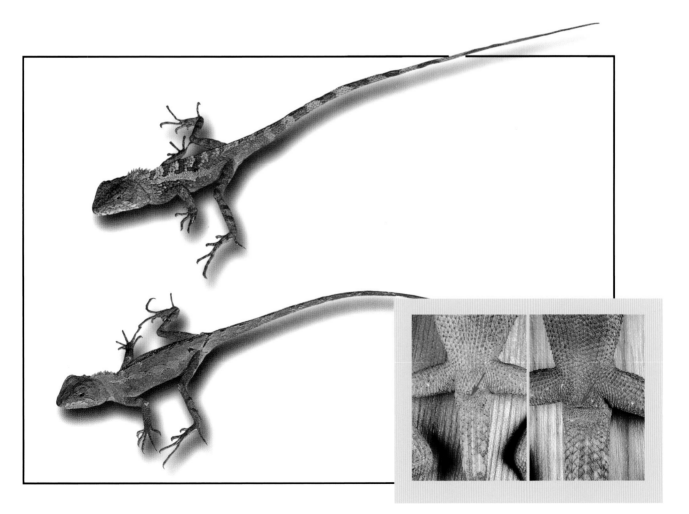

Eggs and Young

Some types of lizards give birth to live young. Others carry their eggs in their body until they are ready to hatch. But most lizards lay eggs in a nest. Many females cover their eggs with twigs and leaves to protect them from being eaten.

Lizard eggshells are usually tough and leathery. Babies have a special egg tooth on their snout. They use it to help split open their shell when it is time to hatch.

After breaking out of its shell, a baby lizard pushes its way out of the nest, and up to the surface. The egg tooth disappears soon after.

Hatchlings on Their Own

Baby lizards are called hatchlings. Most lizard mothers do not stay and raise their hatchlings. Once out of its nest, a hatchling has to find its own way in the world.

Baby lizards are able to find food by themselves right away. Some hatchlings help each other until they grow a bit older. Many others fight to get the food they need.

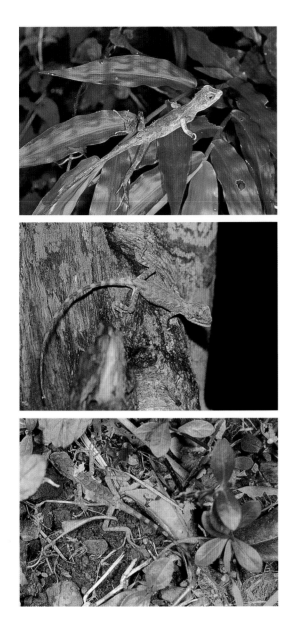

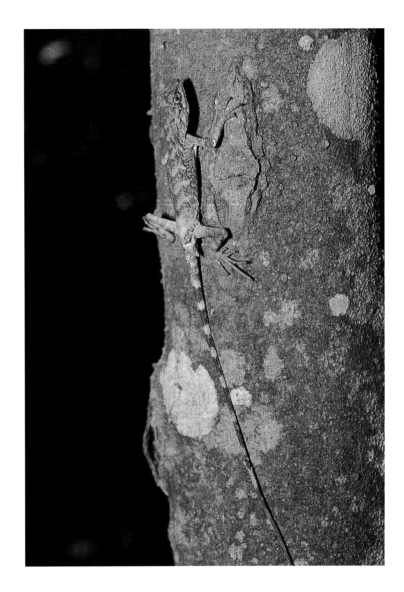

Defenses and Survival

Many kinds of birds, snakes, and mammals eat lizards. Most lizards use speed to escape an enemy. Some large lizards fight back by biting. Others try to scare off attackers by puffing up their necks, hissing, or spitting. Some lizards stay out of danger by blending into the background.

Most lizards can even lose their tail to break free! If an enemy grabs a lizard by the tail, the lizard can let its tail snap off. This keeps the attacker busy as the lizard sneaks away. The tail usually grows back within a year.

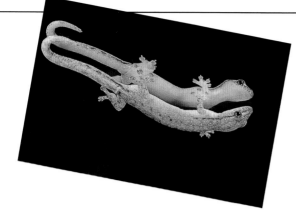

The Amazing Variety of Lizards

Lizards come in an amazing variety of shapes, sizes, and colors.

Lizards make up the largest group of reptiles. There are more than 3,500 different kinds of lizards in the world. Many of these are skinks. Skinks have smooth scales and shiny bodies. Geckos are the best climbers. And monitors are the largest lizards in the world. Each kind of lizard holds a special place in the animal kingdom.

For More Information

Kalman, Bobbie. *What Is a Reptile?* St. Catharine's, ON: Crabtree Publishing, 1999.

Matero, Robert. *Lizards (Eyes on Nature).* Chicago, IL: Kidsbooks, 1997.

Trueit, Trudi Strain. *Lizards (True Books: Animals).* Danbury, CT: Childrens Press, 2003.

Glossary

cloaca the opening to a lizard's reproductive system

hatchling a baby lizard

prey an animal that is food for another animal